You Can Have Mountain Moving Faith

You Can Have Mountain Moving Faith

Practical Steps to Realizing God's Promises in Your Life

Johnathan Wallace

Book design by eBook Prep
www.ebookprep.com

December 2022
ISBN: 978-1-64457-590-1

Rise UP Publications
644 Shrewsbury Commons Ave
Ste 249
Shrewsbury PA 17361
United States of America
www.riseUPpublications.com
Phone: 866-846-5123

Contents

Introduction

I am writing this during the COVID-19 "pandemic." Yes, I say that sarcastically because it is early September, and it is hardly a pandemic in the natural world and most definitely not in the spiritual world. The numbers are dropping, and the ones that "stand" are proving false.

The only thing that remains true is the Word of God. The true plague has shown its face. It's not a disease passed by the sniffles or shaking someone's hand. It is a spiritual rot circulated from the pulpits around the world. Jesus called it the yeast of the Pharisees. Jesus told us to be on guard or beware of it. The problem may not be in what is taught; it's more in what's not being taught. We have seen leaders shut their doors to host "online church" where they preach about baking cookies and not killing your quarantined kids. I am not trying to dishonor the Bride of Christ; I am simply exposing a demonic spirit known as fear and unbelief plaguing the Church of the Lord. Tests reveal where you are proficient and where you are deficient. The Lord does not tempt us; that is the Devil's work. What we do when he comes to kill, steal, and destroy is the gauge of our faith.

Our faith is not determined by what we claim in Donald Trump's 2019 roaring economy. Our faith is determined by what we do when staring at a fiery furnace and it's time to act. Do we bow, or do we stand?

Many things have been exposed during this season, from a sex trafficking ring in Hollywood to the blatant demonic agendas of the leftist liberals. The hidden things are now coming to light.

This is a year of exposure. Jeremiah Johnson said, "The Devil has been caught with his hand in the cookie jar." You don't need to ask the Lord what He wants us to teach when you can read the exam papers for yourself and see what people are getting wrong. If seventy percent of the class got an "F", it is not time to move on. It is a sign of misunderstanding or ignorance.

I want to help with this issue. I do not want to shame the Bride of Christ; I would be shaming myself. I want to help you understand the most basic principle in the Bible, the simple doctrine of faith.

Together we will see a mighty end-time revival, where faith comes alive in the people of God, and we see this country shaken by the power of the Holy Spirit.

Chapter One

Why is Faith Important?

Therefore, leaving the discussion of the elementary principles of Christ, let us go on to perfec-
tion, not laying again the foundation of
repentance from dead works and of faith
toward God.

— Hebrews 6:1 NLT

The Bible calls faith an elementary principle. Many people talk like deep philosophers and profound theologians, but they are not people of faith. People claim spiritual maturity or superiority but are nothing more than book scholars. The Bible is not only a book to be annotated or discussed. The Bible is to be lived and experienced. You cannot run before you walk. You cannot do calculus if you don't know simple addition. You can't have anything or do anything in the Lord until you learn the lesson of faith. A house is not built before the foundation.

Faith is the foundation. It is the first lesson you must learn. For reasons beyond me, we have moved away from and are not teaching people the message of faith. Therefore, when tested by difficulties, millions fail because they didn't go to a church that taught them the fundamental tenets of Christianity.

Faith is not a minor doctrine, or something seldom mentioned in the scriptures. The word "faith" appears hundreds of times. When you extend the search to synonyms for faith, like "believe" or even passages that illustrate faith in the context, the results are enormous. Faith is like water. Without water, you have no life. Without faith, you have no connection to God whatsoever.

> And it is impossible to please God without faith.
> Anyone who wants to come to him must
> believe that God exists and that he rewards
> those who sincerely seek him.
>
> — Hebrews 11:6 NLT

> That you may walk worthy of the Lord, fully
> pleasing Him being fruitful in every good work
> and increasing in the knowledge of God;
>
> — Colossians 1:10 NLT

You cannot please God without faith. Every Christian should unanimously agree, despite theological persuasion, that, according to Colossians 1:10, our collective goal is to please God.

Anyone with a rational mind agrees with that conclusion. The Bible then tells us that without faith it is impossible to please Him (Hebrews 11:16).

This is why faith is fundamental; it's the ABC's of Christianity. God isn't looking for the smartest individuals. God isn't only interested in people who can quote chapters and verses of the scriptures by memory. Those things are wonderful, but if a person does not have faith, they are not pleasing God. Faith is what pleases God. It's so simple. God wants faith.

> For by grace you have been saved through faith,
> and that not of yourselves; it is the gift of God
>
> — Ephesians 2:8 NLT

Salvation is the single most important tenet of Christianity. The Bible says that faith is how you receive the salvation that was purchased for you by the blood of Jesus. Do you see why faith is so important? It is only by faith that you have salvation. If you don't have salvation, you will not inherit the Kingdom of God. You will never access one thing from God during your life on Earth. Salvation is the beginning point; it is the death of your old life and the rebirth of your new life full of the promises of God. Salvation is step one.

The Bible says that it's by faith that you are saved. If people don't understand faith, how can anyone even be saved? People misunderstand faith. Without it, you can't please God, you can't be saved, and you can't receive anything from the Lord.

Anything that was ever done in the Bible was done by faith. If they needed faith to do what they did, why do we think we can do it apart from faith? Our own intellect and ability, apart from Christ, can accomplish nothing of eternal value. Read the passage below.

> Faith shows the reality of what we hope for; it is the evidence of things we cannot see. Through their faith, the people in days of old earned a good reputation.
> By faith we understand that the entire universe was formed at God's command, that what we now see did not come from anything that can be seen.
> It was by faith that Abel brought a more acceptable offering to God than Cain did. Abel's offering gave evidence that he was a righteous man, and God showed his approval of his gifts. Although Abel is long dead, he still speaks to us by his example of faith.
> It was by faith that Enoch was taken up to heaven without dying—"he disappeared, because God took him." For before he was taken up, he was known as a person who pleased God. And it is impossible to please God without faith. Anyone who wants to come to him must believe that God exists and that he rewards those who sincerely seek him.
> It was by faith that Noah built a large boat to save his family from the flood. He obeyed God,

who warned him about things that had never happened before. By his faith Noah condemned the rest of the world, and he received the righteousness that comes by faith.

It was by faith that Abraham obeyed when God called him to leave home and go to another land that God would give him as his inheritance. He went without knowing where he was going. And even when he reached the land God promised him, he lived there by faith— for he was like a foreigner, living in tents. And so did Isaac and Jacob, who inherited the same promise. Abraham was confidently looking forward to a city with eternal foundations, a city designed and built by God.

It was by faith that even Sarah was able to have a child, though she was barren and was too old. She believed[b] that God would keep his promise. And so a whole nation came from this one man who was as good as dead—a nation with so many people that, like the stars in the sky and the sand on the seashore, there is no way to count them.

All these people died still believing what God had promised them. They did not receive what was promised, but they saw it all from a distance and welcomed it. They agreed that they were foreigners and nomads here on earth. Obviously people who say such things are looking forward to a country they can call their own. If they had longed for the country they came from, they could have gone back. But they were looking for a better place, a heavenly homeland. That is why God is not ashamed to be called their God, for he has prepared a city for them.

It was by faith that Abraham offered Isaac as a sacrifice when God was testing him. Abraham, who had received God's promises, was ready to sacrifice his only son, Isaac, even though God had told him, "Isaac is the son through whom your descendants will be counted." Abraham reasoned that if Isaac died, God was able to bring him back to life again. And in a sense, Abraham did receive his son back from the dead.

It was by faith that Isaac promised blessings for the future to his sons, Jacob and Esau.

It was by faith that Jacob, when he was old and dying, blessed each of Joseph's sons and bowed in worship as he leaned on his staff.

It was by faith that Joseph, when he was about to die, said confidently that the people of Israel would leave Egypt. He even commanded them to take his bones with them when they left.

It was by faith that Moses' parents hid him for three months when he was born. They saw that God had given them an unusual child, and they were not afraid to disobey the king's command.

It was by faith that Moses, when he grew up,
refused to be called the son of Pharaoh's
daughter. He chose to share the oppression of
God's people instead of enjoying the fleeting
pleasures of sin. He thought it was better to
suffer for the sake of Christ than to own the
treasures of Egypt, for he was looking ahead to
his great reward. It was by faith that Moses
left the land of Egypt, not fearing the king's
anger. He kept right on going because he kept
his eyes on the one who is invisible. It was by
faith that Moses commanded the people of
Israel to keep the Passover and to sprinkle
blood on the doorposts so that the angel of
death would not kill their firstborn sons.

It was by faith that the people of Israel went right
through the Red Sea as though they were on
dry ground. But when the Egyptians tried to
follow, they were all drowned.

It was by faith that the people of Israel marched
around Jericho for seven days, and the walls
came crashing down.

It was by faith that Rahab the prostitute was not
destroyed with the people in her city who
refused to obey God. For she had given a
friendly welcome to the spies.

How much more do I need to say? It would take
too long to recount the stories of the faith of
Gideon, Barak, Samson, Jephthah, David,
Samuel, and all the prophets. By faith these

> people overthrew kingdoms, ruled with justice,
> and received what God had promised them.
> They shut the mouths of lions, quenched the
> flames of fire, and escaped death by the edge
> of the sword. Their weakness was turned to
> strength. They became strong in battle and put
> whole armies to flight.
>
> — Hebrews 11:1-34 NLT

Prayers are meant to be answered. They are not supposed to hit the ceiling and return void. Let me ask you a question: What are you hoping for? Financial increase? Healing? A reconciled marriage? A wayward child? What are the things you desire? Faith is what those miracles are made from.

I once saw a vision where the Lord showed me practically how faith works and why it is so important. I saw myself thinking out loud, "it sure would be nice if." The prayer for the thing I was hoping for floated up to Heaven. God received it and said, "Yes, this is good; I would love to do this for my son. It is my will for my son to have this." I then saw God walk over to this basket with the name materials/substance_written on the side. He reached into the basket to grab the materials to create the thing I was hoping for, but the basket was empty. There was no faith, no substance. So, God wasn't able to create what I was hoping for.

Faith was the fabric from which my miracle was to be made. Without faith, God has no material to build with. God can't create something from nothing. Faith is the material by which the world came into existence. Faith is what your miracle is made of. We have only scratched the surface of the infinite importance of faith. You can see why it is so important that every believer understands faith and intentionally exercises it. So, what is faith? How do I get it? How do I use it? These are some of the questions I will answer with God's grace and the Holy Spirit's help.

Chapter Two

What is Faith?

When some people talk about faith, it gets confusing. What is faith? If you ask the average Christian that question, you will probably get a confusing answer. They will likely stare at you blankly and say, "Faith is hoping for the best." That's hope, not faith. If you do not know what faith is, you will never use or possess faith.

The world dictionary defines faith as the following: "Complete trust or confidence in someone or something." It's that simple. Faith, in our context, is complete confidence and trust in the Lord. Do not overcomplicate it. The Bible is not filled with deep-thinking theologians. It is filled with stories of everyday men and women who understand He is who He says He is and will do what He says He will do.

> Elijah was as human as we are, and yet when he
> prayed earnestly that no rain would fall, none
> fell for three and a half years!
>
> —James 5:17 NLT

Elijah was a man who believed God was who He said He was and would do what He said He would do. What were the results of taking God at His Word? Many miracles. Looking at people in the Bible like superheroes possessing great abilities is easy. But they weren't special in themselves.

It wasn't the average joes who were great; they just took God at His word. You see, faith is not "I hope this happens." That is not faith because, in your mind, there is still a chance it won't happen. A "that would be nice" mindset is not faith. Faith is having something settled inside of you to the degree that you know that you know what God said about the subject is true.

Abraham knew Isaac was the promise fulfilled to the extent he was willing to kill him. If God told him to do so, Abraham believed the Lord would resurrect Isaac from the dead. Abraham was completely convinced; he was sold. Wishful thinking does not produce results. Only what the Bible calls faith produces results.

Many people don't get results because they live with a made-up version of faith, not the absolute certainty and confidence that brings Heaven to Earth. Many people take an "I hope that chair holds me" approach to life. When my wife and I stepped into positions as pastors at our first church, we started with a room full of old blue chairs. They did not match anything, and the welds were coming undone where the legs met the base of the seat. There were times when I straightened the aisles and the chairs would literally collapse with the legs folding in. Many Sundays, I prayed when I saw certain individuals walking in, "Lord, please don't let these chairs fall out from under that man or woman. If they fall on the ground, I don't think we will be able to get them up!"

Faith is an absolute certainty. When the Lord blessed us with newer chairs, I never thought about it again; I knew it wouldn't be a problem. I didn't have to convince myself not to worry. I consciously and subconsciously had confidence that the chairs would support whoever sat in them. Faith is not simply saying something repeatedly while on the inside you are tossed and thrown like a reed in the wind. Faith is coming to the point where you have total confidence, even subconsciously, that God will do what He said in His Word. You can't hope your way through life. You must cross the bridge where you put your complete trust in the Lord and become confident of the things he has said. Faith says have; hope says *will* have.

> "I tell you, you can pray for anything, and if you
> believe that you've received it, it will be yours"
>
> — Mark 11:24 NLT

Jesus told us the key to receiving anything in life. You must believe you have received it. See, many people believe they *will* receive it. That's hope. Hope is the future, faith is now. God is saying the key is not just simply acknowledging that I can or will bring it to you at some future date. The key is seizing the promises of God and deciding that Jesus paid for all 8,000 promises in the Word. All I must do is pick them up. They are at the counter, bought and paid for, all bagged up and ready to go. How do you pick it up? By faith. We will talk about how to use your faith in a practical way a little later on.

One day I was driving to the church and praying to the Lord. At that time, we needed a vehicle. I was praying about the vehicle we needed. The Holy Spirit brought this scripture to mind. He said, "John, do you believe you have that vehicle now?" I said, "Yes, Lord." He then said, "Why don't you act like it?" I didn't know what the Lord meant. He then brought the following scripture to my spirit.

> Then Peter took the lame man by the right hand
> and helped him up. And as he did, the man's
> feet and ankles were instantly healed and
> strengthened. He jumped up, stood on his feet,
> and began to walk! Then, walking, leaping, and
> praising God, he went into the Temple with
> them.
>
> — Acts 3:7-8 NLT

The Lord told me, "This is how someone acts when they receive a miracle." The man was leaping and praising God. When you become sold that you actually possess every blessing He has to give (Ephesians 1:3), all you have to do is truly believe it's already yours to see it come into physical manifestation. You won't have to convince yourself to get excited. You will act like a person who just received a miracle.

I began to holler as if someone had just driven that new vehicle up to my front door. I was thanking the Lord for it! A few months later, we had the vehicle my wife wanted with no loan from a bank! Amen! Faith is believing God!

> Be anxious for nothing, but in everything by
> prayer and supplication, with thanksgiving, let
> your requests be made known to God.
>
> — Philippians 4:6 NKJV

The Bible says to let your requests be made known to God with thanksgiving. That can seem confusing and odd if you don't understand faith. The Bible is talking to someone who knows the promises of God, and truly believes they already belong to the son or daughter through Christ.

When you are not experiencing those promises, begin to claim the promises with your faith by thanking God for what you are entitled to according to the Word (every spiritual blessing). You don't ask for things you already possess; you say "thank you" for them. This is one of many testimonies. I will give you insight into how we saw the Lord bring us a vehicle by our faith. The Lord had planted these scriptures in our hearts during that season.

> The Lord will send rain at the proper time from his rich treasury in the heavens and will bless all the work you do. You will lend to many nations, but you will never need to borrow from them. If you listen to these commands of the Lord your God that I am giving you today, and if you carefully obey them, the Lord will make you the head and not the tail, and you will always be on top and never at the bottom.
>
> — Deuteronomy 28:12-13 NLT

> Just as the rich rule the poor, so the borrower is a servant to the lender.
>
> — Proverbs 22:7 NLT

As a 23-year-old and a 22-year-old, we have only ever lived in a culture that says, "Get a loan if you can't afford it. Just finance it." We live in a generation where people spend money they don't have. They live their life trying to make money, to pay back the money they spent but didn't have in the first place.

Yet we had come across the Word of the Lord. It was on the black and white page. We decided to trust the Lord and wait for the cash to come into our possession to get the vehicle we needed. It seemed impossible, but we were convinced God would do what He said in scripture if we simply believed and obeyed Him.

We went several months without the vehicle. Sometimes, in our flesh, the thought of taking the easy way out crossed our minds.

But we trusted the Lord and stood on His Word. We made the declaration that His Word was true. "Lord, why should we have to go to the world for money? We are children of the King of Kings. Why do we need the help of wicked men and women to have what you promised us in your Word?" We stood in faith and thanked Him for our vehicle.

Sometimes, I wanted to settle for something that my wife didn't want, but she would rebuke me and reassure me that God could give her the vehicle she wanted. "Delight yourself also in the Lord, And He shall give you the desires of your heart." (Psalm 37:4) We did everything we could to stand in faith, and once we did that, we stood some more. Within a matter of weeks, the thousands of dollars we needed came to us from various sources. The day we picked up the vehicle, there was no financing, loan, or credit check, only me counting out the cash and the dealer handing me the title. Believe God at His word and don't settle or compromise!

Our entire lives serving Jesus are filled with testimonies like these. During the winter of 2019, things were shifting at the church plant we were pastoring. We were getting ready to launch in January 2020 as an independent church. The building and property we were operating in belonged to another party. They were initially reluctant to make a deal with us for the property. So, we went to the Word of the Lord.

Look, I am giving all this land to you! Go in and occupy it, for it is the land the Lord swore to give to your ancestors Abraham, Isaac, and Jacob, and to all their descendants.

— Deuteronomy 1:8 NLT

Every place that the sole of your foot will tread upon I have given you, as I said to Moses.

—Joshua 1:3 NLT

So the Lord made a covenant with Abram that day and said, "I have given this land to your descendants, all the way from the border of Egypt to the great Euphrates River—the land now occupied by the Kenites, Kenizzites, Kadmonites, Hittites, Perizzites, Rephaites, Amorites, Canaanites, Girgashites, and Jebusites."

— Genesis 15:18-21 NLT

So all who put their faith in Christ share the same blessing Abraham received because of his faith.

— Galatians 3:9 NLT

The Bible is full of promises to possess the land. God gave land as a part of the blessing to his children in scripture. You cannot read the Bible without promises like these jumping out at you.

The Lord promised land to Abraham, and the Bible says that in Christ, we have received the same promise of blessings as Abraham. If God promised Abraham land as a part of his blessing, He promises you and I land as well.

> In truth I perceive that God shows no partiality.
>
> — Acts 10:34 NLT

The other party told us that the land was on commercial property worth over $400,000. We were a small church of fewer than one hundred people. How could we come up with money like that? We began to stomp our feet on that land (Joshua 1:3). We began to claim our promise in the name of Jesus according to the Word of God. There was talk about us having to relocate and start from scratch at a new location. This was the best property in our little town. It was right off the highway. We had already begun renovating it. The building was equipped to have church services, and our people knew this place as home.

We stood firm on the Word and exercised our faith that God would give us the land we were on. This process was drawn out until, finally, the other party returned and made a deal with us. They said they would sell us the property for ½ of its appraised value. They were expecting $400,000 as an appraisal, so we would have to pay them $200,000. If the story stopped here, that would have been a miracle. Many would have said "Yes, Lord" and gone and got a loan from a bank, but we knew God could do even better.

We continued in fasting and prayer and believed the Lord would deliver this property to us. We would be "the head and not the tail, above and not beneath." Time went on, and the appraisal came back. The commercial property, with half a million dollar lots to the right and left, was appraised at $180,000. It was a miracle! The Lord told the selling party to sell it at half the appraised value, dropping its price to $90,000.

The God of the Bible was answering our prayers! By the time the negotiations were finalized, the selling party said, "Ok, we will do it, but you have to have the money by the end of the month." We started a church that had $800 and 15 people in attendance. The price dropping to $90,000 was a miracle, but we didn't have anything close to that amount. In the flesh, you think "run to the bank next door," but we knew the Word of God, and we continued to pray that God would deliver the property to us.

We had a short time to act, or the deal was off. It's in moments like this that the true test of faith happens. What do you believe? Are you internally convinced? What does one do in a situation where if it doesn't work, you will lose everything?

After much prayer and faith, a member of our church came forward with a check for $97,000; the total price after closing costs. He gave $20,000 as an offering and allowed us to pay him the remainder over a few years at zero percent interest. Praise God! We didn't go through the system that would put money in the Devil's pocket. God used a member of His body to supply the need.

When you stand for God's Word, it stands for you. Faith is simply taking God at His word. He said it. He meant it. He did it. I receive it. Don't overcomplicate faith.

Be like a child. A child believes what they are told. You tell them that a fat man flies around once a year and comes down the chimney to bring them presents, and they believe it. You tell a child that a giant bunny hides eggs around the house on Easter; they believe it. You tell them a fairy takes their baby teeth and exchanges them for a couple of dollars, and they believe it! God said it. I believe it. That is the end of the discussion. The kingdom belongs to those with childlike faith. Why? They are the only ones who will possess it. God is willing to do infinitely more than you can ask, think, or imagine (Ephesians 3:20). Can you believe it?

Chapter Three

The Starting Point

Faith's starting point is accepting God's Word as your absolute authority. If you have not done this, you are like a reed blown and tossed by the wind. If you struggle with believing the Bible as the only truth, you will never possess faith. Faith is forged in the fire. If you are not convinced, you will give up the moment pressure is put on your life. Faith is produced when you stand despite what you see, feel, or experience.

If you are on the fence about truly accepting the Word of God as an absolute authority, you will always live by what you see, think, and experience. You will never see the results of Bible faith. You must conclude that God created the ground you are standing on. He wove the cosmos into existence. He knows more about our world and how it works than we do. He made it. You must take the humble position that He knows what is and what isn't, and what He says goes!

"Heaven and earth will pass away, but My words will by no means pass away."

— Matthew 24:35 NLT

Your word is a lamp to my feet and a light to my path.

— Psalms 119:105 NLT

Faith is being sold on the fact that what God says is final. People say the culture has changed, so we must change the Word. Without the rock-solid foundation of the Word, faith cannot exist. Faith is complete confidence and trust in God by what He has said in His Word. If there is no word, there is no ground to stand on. You have to come to the point where you truly believe that people can change, culture can change, and the world can change, but God's Word is the truth. His Word is your standard, your lamp, your map, and your compass. Your truth is not a book on virtual church growth in the modern world or twenty self-help tips for a better life.

The famous reformer Martin Luther said it best in his confrontation with the Catholic Church. "Sola Scriptura" which means "the scripture alone." There are many decisions in life that you don't have to make because the Bible already made them. All you need to do is accept, believe, and act on it. If, when confronted with the Word of God, you still answer "but," that is a clear indicator that you have not put your trust in the Lord and His Word completely. Until the Word of God becomes your truth, you cannot have Bible faith.

People will say, "I know the Bible says I am healed by his stripes (Isaiah 53:5) BUT..." There can be no "but." That is not faith, and you will never have results. Faith is taking the position that God says I'm healed in His Word. Even if I don't see or feel it, I still believe it and confess it because He said it; therefore, it is true.

People will also say, "I know the Bible says I am the head and not the tail (Deuteronomy 28:13) BUT." That is not faith. If you take that position, then what you see is your authority, what you feel is your authority, but the Word of God is not your authority. The authority of the Bible must trump personal experience in your heart.

Many people struggle because they know the hundreds of promises for healing in the Word of God. Yet, they had a family member who was a devout follower die of a terminal illness. They say, "What do you do with that?" I comfort them. I pray with them. I love them. What happened does not change the Word of God. You cannot let life experience form the truths of the scriptures in your heart. You must allow the scriptures to form how you believe and see the world. This begins with a simple decision. Cross over the bridge today. Invest $15 in a Bible and hold it to Heaven and declare it is true, above all else.

If anything in my life contradicts what is written in this Word, I will choose to believe the Word of God.

Now faith can begin. If you prayed this prayer, you can now begin to use your faith and see the promises of God come to pass in your life.

Chapter Four

How Do I Get Faith?

If faith is the key to life and possessing the promises of God, then how do I obtain faith? In this section, I want to teach you the simple keys and principles to receiving faith and developing your faith.

> So then faith comes by hearing, and hearing by the
> word of God.
>
> — Romans 10:17 NLT

> My people are destroyed for lack of knowledge.
>
> — Hosea 4:6 NLT

We have already discussed the importance of the foundation of the Word of God. Without the Word, there is nothing to stand on. You cannot believe something that you do not know. How can I believe for my body to be healed if I have never read or heard the Word of God regarding healing? How can I be saved if I have never read or heard the Word of God preached about salvation by faith in Jesus Christ?

Faith is possible when you read or hear the Word. As you read the Bible, your mind begins to see all the things available to you. When I was a child, I knew God could save me, but I didn't know the God that gave answers to every area of life.

One day I was reading the Bible and came across the words of Jesus where he said, "I tell you, you can pray for anything, and if you believe that you've received it, it will be yours." (Mark 11:24 NLT) My mind began to explore the infinite possibility of "anything." I said, "Wait, my job is something, my finances are something, my marriage is something." I saw Jesus had promised that if I could believe it, I could have it. Anything! I didn't believe God for many things previously because I didn't know that I could. I didn't know that God had given me provision for all things.

Things were missing in my life that I could have had but "for a lack of knowledge" I did without. Suddenly my mind was open to the reality of "anything" and faith came to believe God for many things I had never believed Him for in the past. Faith comes as you saturate yourself in the Word of God. As you feed on the Word of God daily, your understanding will expand, and you will begin to see the promises you saw before. Then once you see the Word, you have ground to stand on, and you can cling to that Word and see the promises brought into manifestation in your life. Reading the Bible is not a religious duty. It is not an item on the Christian to-do list. Within the pages lies everything you need to prosper and succeed in every area of life.

> It is God's privilege to conceal things and the
> king's privilege to discover them.
>
> — Proverbs 25:2 NLT

All we must do is find the treasures within each page—the nuggets of gold around every corner. Then with childlike faith, we take God at His word and the realities of scripture permeate our lives.

Faith not only comes by reading the Word; it comes by hearing the Word. Two words are used in the Bible for the "Word" of God. First, you have "Logos." We can break this down to mean "the written word of God." These are the words on the pages from Genesis to Revelation. We just discussed the simplicity of reading the "Logos" (the written word). As you read, you are enlightened by the promises extended to you. Then from the "Logos," faith comes for one to believe the promises written on the page.

The other word used in the Bible for the "Word" of God is the word "Rhema." This means "utterance or thing said." This is when God speaks. When God spoke "let there be light," it was the "Rhema," the spoken word of God. Years later, it is in the form of "Logos," the written Word of God.

The key is taking the "Logos" and receiving it as "Rhema." This is, taking the words on the page and having the Holy Spirit speak the Word afresh in your heart. I do not want to confuse you, but both concepts are important for receiving and building faith. "Rhema" is not a thing of the past; God still speaks. He speaks to us today through dreams, visions, prophecy, and the Holy Spirit living on the inside of each believer. When God speaks, the universe is forced to comply with God's spoken word. God said, "Light be," and from the darkness came the cosmos. Jesus told Peter to "come" while walking on water, and the laws of science and physics were forced to comply with God's spoken word, allowing Peter to walk on water. When God speaks a word, that word carries the power to see the command come to pass. When God tells you to "go," the word released carries the provision, anointing, and capacity to see you fulfill the command of God.

> The Lord had said to Abram, "Leave your native country, your relatives, and your father's family, and go to the land that I will show you. I will make you into a great nation. I will bless you and make you famous, and you will be a blessing to others. I will bless those who bless you and curse those who treat you with contempt. All the families on earth will be blessed through you.
>
> — Genesis 12:1-3 NLT

When God spoke this command to Abram, the Word went forth and made the way. Before Abram ever left, there was favor going before him. God was clearing a path ahead of him. God preordained people to cross his path. God was changing the

30

climate of the region He was giving to Abram so that things would naturally flow in his direction.

My wife and I live in deep east Texas. The land is covered in thick woods. If left unattended, the brush will grow so thick with thorns and vines that it becomes nearly impossible to walk through. To create a path, you must get heavy equipment and clear the way. You must cut down the bushes, grind up the stumps, thin out the branches, and cut the grass. This is what happens in the unseen world when God speaks a word; things begin to shift and move. The word released by the Lord goes forth and removes the thorns, the vines, and the obstacles that block your way. All you must do is obey the Holy Spirit, and by faith, walk down the cleared path He has made for you.

> The thief's purpose is to steal and kill and destroy. My purpose is to give them a rich and satisfying life.
>
> —John 10:10 NLT

> The Lord is my shepherd; I have all that I need. He lets me rest in green meadows; he leads me beside peaceful streams. He renews my strength. He guides me along right paths, bringing honor to his name. Even when I walk through the darkest valley, I will not be afraid, for you are close beside me. Your rod and your staff protect and comfort me. You prepare a feast for me in the presence of my enemies. You honor me by anointing my head

with oil. My cup overflows with blessings. Surely
your goodness and unfailing love will pursue me
all the days of my life, and I will live in the house
of the Lord Forever.

— Psalms 23 NLT

The key to success in every area of life is learning to hear the
voice, Rhema of the Holy Spirit, every day. You can trust His
leading because the Bible promises that whatever He tells you to
do, it leads you "to life and life abundantly." Any change He asks
you to make, any turn He tells you to take, any item He tells you
to give is taking you to the place of "still waters, green pastures,
and a cup overflowing with blessings."

I remember the day the Lord told me, "John, I have the best
plan for your life. There is a place I want to take you where your
health is pristine, where my provision flows like water, and my
favor sets you among princes. I know where this place is, and I
know everything in your life that needs to go for you to get
there. Will you trust me?"

When I heard this word, I learned the difference between the
voice of conviction and the voice of condemnation. Conviction
is from the Holy Spirit, and it is from a place of love. Conviction
is when the Holy Spirit places his finger on something because it
is stripping you from the promises of God, and it must go.
Condemnation is from the enemy; it never brings correction. It
is only guilt, shame, and judgment. It is easy to go anywhere and
give anything when you become rooted in the Father's love for
you and His desire to bless you and see you prosper. He doesn't
want you to touch the stove because it will burn you, not

because He wants to strip you from a life of enjoyment. When the Holy Spirit speaks a command to your heart, you can be confident that God has already made it possible. You will walk forward in faith, knowing He goes before you and will never lead you to fall flat on your face. This was the key to Jesus's ministry.

> So Jesus explained, "I tell you the truth, the Son
> can do nothing by himself. He does only what
> he sees the Father doing. Whatever the Father
> does, the Son also does."
>
> — John 5:19 NLT

Jesus never healed one person on His initiative. He only did what the Father, through the vessel of the Holy Spirit, told Him to do. What was the result? Jesus, as a man, simply placed His hands on whomever the Holy Spirit told Him to, and when God tells you to do something, He has already made provision for the command to be carried out. The sick were healed, demons were expelled, and many miracles were done by obedience to the "Rhema" word of God. This is the same model we are to follow in our lives.

> These miraculous signs will accompany those who
> believe: They will cast out demons in my
> name, and they will speak in new languages.
>
> — Mark 16:17 NLT

> But you will receive power when the Holy Spirit
> comes upon you. And you will be my

witnesses, telling people about me everywhere
—in Jerusalem, throughout Judea, in Samaria,
and to the ends of the earth.

— Acts 1:8 NLT

So I say, let the Holy Spirit guide your lives. Then
you won't be doing what your sinful nature
craves.

— Galatians 5:16 NLT

Jesus said all the same signs would follow the believer's life. He said we would receive the power to do these things when we received the Holy Spirit. The gift is not something the Holy Spirit gives you; the gift is the Holy Spirit. You receive the Holy Spirit, and now you can know Him and hear His voice. When He speaks, the anointing and power are given to you to carry out the command. The path is paved, and the miracle is possible by the "Rhema" word of God. Simply let the Holy Spirit guide your life, and signs, wonders, and miracles will follow.

We cannot simply make our path. For the Lord to go before us, He must first give the command. Every promise in the Bible is available to you. But before it produces fruit, you must have the Holy Spirit personally speak the word into your life and situation. God cannot bring life to a word that is not in your mind or spirit. You must read the Word of God and become thoroughly acquainted with the Bible for the Holy Spirit to bring the word in your heart to life.

Many people see an extreme lack in their lives regarding the promises of God. Yet they are severely ignorant regarding the promises available to them. You must first see or hear the Word to receive it by faith. Now to flip the coin, knowing the Bible apart from the Holy Spirit produces no fruit except for the governing laws that God has set in place. Many spiritual laws in the Bible will work when obeyed intentionally or unintentionally simply because God created the unseen world to function according to spiritual and physical laws.

One example is the law of sowing and reaping. "Do not be deceived, God is not mocked; for whatever a man sows, that he will also reap." (Galatians 6:7 NKJV) This principle will work for anyone saved or unsaved because it is a law that governs the world that God created. Some call it karma, but a believer knows this principle as the law of sowing and reaping. If a word (Logos) from God is not quickened to you by the Holy Spirit to become (Rhema), there is no grace available for the Word to be fulfilled.

The Pharisees were required to have the entire Old Testament memorized, yet they were referred to as "whitewashed tombs" by Jesus. They were well-versed in the scriptures yet far from God. You can know with your mind the "Logos," but faith doesn't work from your mind; it can only come from your heart.

> That if you confess with your mouth the Lord
> Jesus and believe in your heart that God has
> raised Him from the dead, you will be saved.
>
> — Romans 10:9 NKJV

You can't simply believe in your mind; Bible faith comes from the heart. The Holy Spirit takes the written Word and whispers it to your heart. The curtain of a man's soul must be opened, and must receive revelation from the Holy Spirit. Only the Holy Spirit can do this.

> When Jesus came into the region of Caesarea
> Philippi, He asked His disciples, saying, "Who
> do men say that I, the Son of Man, am?" So
> they said, "Some say John the Baptist, some
> Elijah, and others Jeremiah or one of the
> prophets." He said to them, "But who do you
> say that I am?" Simon Peter answered and said,
> "You are the Christ, the Son of the living
> God." Jesus answered and said to him, "Blessed
> are you, Simon Bar-Jonah, for flesh and blood
> has not revealed this to you, but My Father
> who is in heaven.
>
> — Matthew 16:13-17 NKJV

Jesus's identity was not a secret, but there was a shift when the information went from Peter's head to Peter's heart. The Holy Spirit revealed the truth to Peter's heart. Jesus was God in the flesh. Faith in Christ as the Messiah came with the gentle "Rhema" whisper of the Holy Spirit.

Now the question is, "How can I get the Holy Spirit to speak to me?" We have already discussed that you must have the Word in you for the Holy Spirit to breathe life into it. To recognize the voice of the Holy Spirit, you must know how the Holy Spirit speaks.

A Still and Small Voice

> Your own ears will hear him. Right behind you a
> voice will say, "This is the way you should go,"
> whether to the right or to the left.
>
> — Isaiah 30:21 NLT

> My sheep listen to my voice; I know them, and
> they follow me.
>
> —John 10:27 NLT

The Holy Spirit is as real as every person you have ever encountered. He exists not in the seen world but in the unseen world.

> For through him God created everything in the
> heavenly realms and on earth. He made the
> things we can see and the things we can't see—
> such as thrones, kingdoms, rulers, and authori-
> ties in the unseen world. Everything was
> created through him and for him.
>
> — Colossians 1:16 NLT

An entire world exists that is equally as real as the world you perceive. These two worlds exist together simultaneously. Yet you cannot see in the spiritual world with physical eyes, and you cannot hear in the spiritual world with physical ears. Only by the revelation gifts of the Spirit (1 Corinthians 12:7-11) can you see and hear in the spiritual realm. My point is, many people miss the voice of the Holy Spirit because they are looking for Him in the wrong place.

God can speak audibly; He spoke audibly in the Bible. Messenger angels can appear to people. An angel appeared to Paul to bring confidence that Paul and the ship's crew would not perish in the storm (Acts 27). God will speak through dreams and visions. This happened many times in the New Testament to give specific instruction and direction (Acts:10). All these things are possible, but most of the time God's everyday instruction will come through the voice of the Holy Spirit. How can I hear this voice?

> Don't you realize that your body is the temple of the Holy Spirit, who lives in you and was given to you by God? You do not belong to yourself,"
>
> — 1 Corinthians 6:19 NKJV

> And I will put my Spirit in you so that you will follow my decrees and be careful to obey my regulations.
>
> — Ezekiel 36:27 NKJV

> For God wanted them to know that the riches and glory of Christ are for you Gentiles, too. And

this is the secret: Christ lives in you. This gives
you assurance of sharing his glory.

— Colossians 1:27 NKJV

There are diversities of gifts, but the same Spirit.
There are differences of ministries, but the
same Lord. And there are diversities of activi-
ties, but it is the same God who works all in
all. But the manifestation of the Spirit to each
one for the profit of all: for to one is given
the word of wisdom through the Spirit, to
another the word of knowledge through the
same Spirit, to another faith by the same
Spirit, to another gifts of healings by the same
Spirit, to another the working of miracles, to
another prophecy, to another discerning of
spirits, to another different kinds of tongues,
to another the interpretation of tongues. But
one and the same Spirit works all these
things, distributing to each one individually as
He wills.

— 1 Corinthians 12:4-11 NKJV

You must first understand that a gift cannot be learned or
taught; it can only be caught. There are many things that people
have a natural ability to do. When people think of having a gift,
they think of singing, playing an instrument, drawing, or something similar. Many skills develop by the focus and practice of
the human mind, but these are not what the Bible calls "gifts of

the Holy Spirit." The Holy Spirit gives a person supernatural "abilities," not only natural abilities.

The ability to prophesy the future is not natural; it is supernatural. The ability to read a person's thoughts is not natural; it is supernatural. The ability to heal the sick is not natural; it is supernatural. These are works of the Holy Spirit done through a person who is the human vessel. The "gift" is not God giving you a skill; the gift is the Holy Spirit (Luke 11:13).

When you receive the Holy Spirit, He manifests His power through your life in a way that is specific to the need presented and specific to your assignment. When God wants something done on the earth, He uses a man or a woman. Christ is the head, and we are the body. The head is not designed for carrying out tasks. The head is the mind that sends the signal to the body. When a door needs to be opened, the head tells the hand, and the hand opens the door. We are the hands, feet, minds, and mouths that He uses.

You cannot earn the way Holy Spirit manifests through your life because He "works all these things as He wills." The Bible says there is a gift, a manifestation called faith, that is a work of the Holy Spirit. When God needs something done and faith to move His hand, the Holy Spirit will manifest faith through a man or a woman to accomplish His will.

Chapter Five

What is the Gift of Faith?

So Jesus answered and said to them, "Have faith in
God. For assuredly, I say to you, whoever says
to this mountain, 'Be removed and be cast into
the sea,' and does not doubt in his heart, but
believes that those things he says will be done,
he will have whatever he says."

— Mark 11:22-23 NLT

In this passage, Jesus talks about the gift of faith. In a
modern translation, we read the words "have faith in God,"
but the original translation of this passage is "have the faith of
God." Having faith *in* God and having the faith *of* God are two
different things. How can I have the faith of God? This is the
gift of faith or the manifestation of faith by the Holy Spirit. This
is God's faith working through you. The passage above gives us
insight into what God's faith really is. "Does not doubt in his

heart." The gift of faith is the absolute assurance with no human doubt whatsoever. If there is doubt, it is not the supernatural gift of faith.

This is not 99.9% faith and 0.1% doubt. This is God's faith. God didn't doubt when he said, "Let there be light." God didn't close His eyes and cross His fingers and toes as He spoke the world into existence. He knew everything that proceeded from His mouth would come to pass. This was the same faith that Jesus operated in. Jesus was God in the flesh; therefore, He had God's faith.

> He noticed a fig tree in full leaf a little way off, so
> he went over to see if he could find any figs.
> But there were only leaves because it was too
> early in the season for fruit. Then Jesus said to
> the tree, "May no one ever eat your fruit
> again!" And the disciples heard him say it.
>
> — Mark 11:13-14

Jesus cursed the fig tree and continued on His journey. He didn't stand around and wait to see what happened; He didn't need to. He knew that whatever came out of His mouth would come to pass. There was no question in His mind. Jesus continued to Jerusalem and passed by the same location the next day.

> The next morning as they passed by the fig tree he
> had cursed, the disciples noticed it had with-
> ered from the roots up. Peter remembered
> what Jesus had said to the tree on the previous

day and exclaimed, "Look, Rabbi! The fig tree
you cursed has withered and died!"

— Mark 11:20-21 NLT

This is the gift of faith; this is God's faith. When he spoke, it came to pass with no exceptions. His faith was Him knowing that what He said would happen with no exceptions. "Take up your mat and walk. Be healed. Lazarus, come out." When Jesus spoke these things, he knew that each miracle would happen. How did He know? By faith in the Word of God.

> The scroll of Isaiah the prophet was handed to
> him. He unrolled the scroll and found the
> place where this was written: "The Spirit of
> the Lord is upon me, for he has anointed me to
> bring Good News to the poor. He has sent me
> to proclaim that captives will be released, that
> the blind will see, that the oppressed will be
> set free, and that the time of the Lord's favor
> has come."

— Luke 4:17-19 NLT

Jesus knew His assignment from the Father. The Lord had revealed to Jesus that the words the prophet Isaiah spoke in chapter 61, verses 1 through 2, were speaking prophetically about Him. When Jesus was baptized, and the heavens opened, and the Holy Spirit descended upon Him like a dove, He knew at that moment that he had received the power and ability to bring Good News to the poor, proclaim that captives will be released, heal the sick and the blind, release the oppressed and preach the Lord's favor.

When He spoke to the blind, He knew in His heart that the Father had given Him the anointing of the Holy Spirit to heal the blind. So, if He gave the command, it would certainly come to pass. By His faith He did signs, wonders, and miracles. The gift of faith is when you know your words are as good as God's. When you speak, it must happen with no exceptions. What you bless must be blessed. What you curse must be cursed. What you command will happen—no ifs, ands, or buts.

This is what it means to have the faith of God. This is the supernatural gift of faith. This is how the Holy Spirit manifests faith through a believer. This is not something you can train yourself in. This is not something you can fake or force. The Holy Spirit will work in this way, through you, if you have yielded and faith is needed.

The first meeting I was invited to preach at was in Idaho. The Lord supernaturally opened a door for me to preach during three days of meetings. When my wife and I were invited, we knew we should go. God had told me I would go to this church many months before any invitation came. We had it marked on the calendar, but we needed the money for two roundtrip plane tickets from Texas to Idaho; we didn't have it then.

One day, I was in my living room, and the Holy Spirit told me to go outside and pray. As I walked outside, I began to pray in the Spirit. As I was praying, I felt faith rise inside of me. This experience is not something explainable, it must be experienced. It was like a bubbling spring, and as it burst forth from my mouth, I said the words, "tickets come forth in Jesus' name." I prayed for the things the Lord had laid on my heart and then went on with my business.

That night we were at our Thursday night prayer meeting at the church. Ten minutes before the prayer meeting started, I was sitting in my office preparing. Suddenly I got a message on my phone to look at my email. I quickly opened my email and saw two plane tickets from Texas to Idaho sitting in my inbox. A loved one who knew nothing of my prayers or situation was praying, and the Lord told them to buy two plane tickets from Texas to Idaho for my wife and me. I had received a miracle! When a need arose, and God wanted to get something into my hand, the Holy Spirit gave me the "faith of God," and I commanded those tickets to come into my possession.

This has happened many times since then. When my wife and I had taken our first church as senior pastors, there was little to no money in the church account. The first week we were instated, we met an $800 water bill because someone had left a toilet running for a month prior. That was all the money in the entire account. We had electricity to pay, workers to pay, and we also had to eat. The tithes the first few weeks were little to none, only a few hundred dollars here and there.

I remember reading a book by Kenneth E. Hagin called "You Can Have What You Say." In this book, he talks about angels sent to serve those who will inherit salvation (Hebrews 1:14). He said angels could be sent forth with the command to gather the things that belong to you. When I read these words, I felt the faith of God bubbling inside of me. Like a fountain, the words came out of my mouth: "Servant Angels, I command you to bring forth $2,000 a week from this point forward." I would never have spoken to God's angels like that, but the faith of God was manifesting through me. $2,000 a week doesn't sound like a lot to many, but it was a tremendous amount more than what this church had ever produced before. That next week the tithes jumped from $300 to $4,000! The angels actually gave me a double portion. From that week, the tithes never dropped below $2,000. When God speaks, it must come to pass. The gift of faith is the faith of God. This is a manifestation of the Holy Spirit available to all believers.

What Does the Gift of Faith Do?

> Then Jesus said to the disciples, "Have faith in
> God. I tell you the truth, you can say to this
> mountain, 'May you be lifted up and thrown
> into the sea,' and it will happen. But you must
> really believe it will happen and have no doubt
> in your heart. I tell you, you can pray for
> anything, and if you believe that you've
> received it, it will be yours.
>
> — Mark 11:22-24 NLT

There are two specific things I want to pull out of this passage. The gift of faith is given to move the mountains in your life. So many people think Christianity is taking a hike through the mountains and valleys. You go up and down, round and round. "You can't appreciate the mountain top without first going through the valley, Amen?" No! Jesus didn't tell his disciples to take a hike when a mountain stood in their way. He said, "Speak to the mountain and command it to be removed, and if you have faith, it will be done." The gift of faith is for moving mountains, slaying Goliaths, and shutting the mouths of lions.

When Peter was held in prison in Acts 12, the faith of the Church didn't give Peter the comfort to get through a hard time. The faith of a praying church caused an angel of the Lord to appear to Peter, the shackles to fall off, and Peter to walk out the front door. When you have the gift of faith, nothing is impossible. This is the bigger picture that Jesus illustrated; moving a physical mountain is impossible. There is no human power or force that can pick up a mountain in its entirety and move it out of the way. If you have the faith of God, the gift of faith, you can speak to a mountain like God, and it will be lifted up and removed.

Get this in your spirit today. Nothing is impossible for the one who believes. Get out of the realm of human reasoning and take God at His Word. You can have what your faith says you can have. You can do what your faith says you can do. If your faith says yes, God will never say no. This passage specifically says that the gift of faith is for moving mountains.

It also says that the gift of faith is for bringing anything and all things into your possession. "You can pray for anything, and if you believe that you've received it, it will be yours." How big is anything? The King James translation reads, "Therefore I say unto you, What things soever ye desire, when ye pray, believe that ye receive them, and ye shall have them." The Greek word used here for "what" is the word "hosos." It means "as great as, as far as, how much, how many, whoever." This means there is no limit to the quantity or quality of what you can have and ask our Father for.

The next word is "things." The Greek word here is "pas," meaning "each, every, any, all, the whole, everyone, all things, everything." You can have anything, and not only can you have anything, but there is also no limit to the quantity and quality of "whatsoever you desire." The gift of faith brings these specific things into your life. If you have the faith of God, you can move any obstacle that stands in front of you, and you can call any and all things forth in your life!

How Can I Get the Gift of Faith?

Right now, we are addressing the gift of faith. This is different from faith which is developed or acquired over time. Faith comes from hearing and reading the Word of God, Logos, and Rhema. This is a supernatural manifestation like the other nine gifts of the Spirit. It is also received just like the other nine gifts of the Spirit. To receive the gift of faith, you must know how the gifts of the Spirit work and are acquired.

As we covered before, the gift is not an ability God gives you. The gift is the Holy Spirit. What we call the gifts of the Spirit are simply the Holy Spirit working through a believer in a specific way according to the need presented or the calling and purpose of that believer. You won't get stuck putting God in a box if you understand this.

People think they are limited to one specific gift or ability. Jesus operated in every single "gift" listed in 1 Corinthians 12 except for Tongues and Interpretation. Even with that, some studies might say otherwise—that is another message for another time. When you see that it's not abilities that are given, but the Spirit Himself ministering through you as a vessel, you will realize the capacity to operate in all nine gifts of the Spirit. It's not about getting an ability from God; it's about yielding to what the Holy Spirit wants to do in and through you.

If a person is sick, God is a healer and lives inside of you. If you yield, you can flow in the gift of healing. If God wants to speak a word and you are the only one who has yielded to His voice in a given setting, you will operate in the gift of prophecy. If a mountain needs to be moved, or a promise needs to come into manifestation, and you're the only believer present, you will operate in the gift of faith if you have yielded.

The Holy Spirit works to meet needs. If you want to operate in a gift of the Spirit, put yourself in a position for Him to use you. The Holy Spirit isn't given so you can sit on your couch and get butterflies while watching television and scrolling through Facebook. The Holy Spirit is given for you to carry on the ministry of Jesus Christ.

> "The Spirit of the Lord is upon Me, Because He has anointed Me To preach the gospel to the poor; He has sent Me to heal the brokenhearted, To proclaim liberty to the captives And recovery of sight to the blind, To set at liberty those who are oppressed; To proclaim the acceptable year of the Lord."
>
> — Luke 4:18-19 NKJV

Begin preaching to the poor. Pursue the brokenhearted. Minister to those bound by the Devil. Lay your hands on the sick, and you will see the Holy Spirit supernaturally manifesting through your life. You have the entire Holy Spirit, not 10% and not 50%. You have 100% of the Holy Spirit. It is not trying to get more from God. It is recognizing what you have by faith and then yielding to the Holy Spirit.

> But covet earnestly the best gifts: and yet shew I
> unto you a more excellent way.
>
> — 1 Corinthians 12:31 KJV

> "However, this kind does not go out except by
> prayer and fasting."
>
> — Matthew 17:21 NKJV

These two scriptures give us insight into how to see a manifestation of the Holy Spirit in your life when you are currently not seeing it. "Covet earnestly the best gifts." The word "covet" used here is the Greek word "zēloō" and it means "to burn with zeal, to desire one earnestly, to strive after, busy one's self about him." The Bible says that if you are not seeing the Holy Spirit work through you in a specific way, you can pursue that specific manifestation.

You can set your eyes on any of the nine gifts and pursue that gift with burning zeal. You are not trying to get God to give you something you don't have; in reality, you are removing blockages preventing you from yielding to the Holy Spirit in that area.

What will happen if you begin to zealously pursue healing? You will begin to follow others that see people healed. You will begin to "pray and fast" (Matthew 17:21) regarding healing. You will begin stepping out in faith and laying your hands on the sick. Most of the time, people are not used because they are not putting themselves in a position to be used. Some may say, "God doesn't heal people through me." But the question is, "how many people have you laid hands on for healing? Set your faith for God to use you in that way. Consecrate yourself to a specific area. Then, after consecration, you learn how to yield to the Holy Spirit in that area of your life, and you begin to see supernatural results.

This is true for the gift of faith. Begin praying for the Holy Spirit to give you a supernatural revelation of faith. Begin consecrating yourself to God by fasting and get rid of worldly blockages in your life. Zealously pursue the manifestation of faith. Read books by Kenneth E. Hagin and Smith Wigglesworth and begin seeing the Holy Spirit move in you and through you in that way. Mountains will move, and miracles will begin springing forth.

Chapter Six

How Do I Use My Faith?

I t does you no good to have all the faith in the world if you do not know how to use your faith. Many people hold the Word of God very dear in their hearts and yet never see the supernatural in their lives. This is because their faith is bottled up, with the lid tightly sealed. They must let it out for it to work. I want to teach you simple principles that guarantee results. The Bible teaches us clearly how to get our faith to produce actual fruit in our lives.

Speak

> Then Jesus said to the disciples, "Have faith in
> God. I tell you the truth, you can say to this
> mountain, 'May you be lifted up and thrown
> into the sea,' and it will happen. But you must
> really believe it will happen and have no doubt

in your heart. I tell you, you can pray for
anything, and if you believe that you've
received it, it will be yours."

— Mark 11:22-24 NLT

This is simple, yet people never learn this basic principle. How
did Jesus say to move the mountain? Think in your head? Wish
in your heart? No! He said, "Say." You must speak to the mountain for it to move. If you don't speak, it won't move. You can
have all the faith in the world in your heart, but if you don't put
your faith into action by speaking, it remains dormant and
produces nothing.

You must be rooted in the Word of God; again, this is where
faith comes from. Then from your knowledge of what the Bible
says, and your trust in its truth, you speak and command the
promises of God's Word to come to pass in your life and situation. If you are struggling with cancer, do not sit and wish God
would do something about it. You will die if you do that. You
have the authority; therefore, you must speak.

"Look, I have given you authority over all the
power of the enemy, and you can walk among
snakes and scorpions and crush them. Nothing
will injure you."

— Luke 10:19 NLT

If a new restaurant opens in our hometown of Lufkin, Texas, the
franchise will send a manager to get the restaurant up and

running. This manager carries the authority to hire and fire, direct and call the shots. What would happen if every time the manager was pressed to make a decision, he just threw up his hands and said, "Let's wait until the owner does something." The store would close in a week, and that manager would be fired.

Jesus has given us authority. He has appointed us as managers of His kingdom on Earth. We must speak and command the mountains to move. If you have sickness or disease in your body, command it to leave using the name of Jesus. Say, "Cancer, I curse you in Jesus' name. You must leave my body now and never return again. I will live and not die. I will live and prosper in the land the Lord has given me." Say, "Father, you promise me long life according to Psalm 91:16 and Ephesians 6:3, so therefore this sickness will not take me out. I cannot die. I will not die in Jesus' name."

You must speak and command things into existence. When your finances are tested, say, "Father, you said, 'Oh, the joys of those who do not follow the advice of the wicked, or stand around with sinners, or join in with mockers. But they delight in the law of the Lord, meditating on it day and night. They are like trees planted along the riverbank, bearing fruit each season, Their leaves never wither, and they prosper in all they do.' (Psalm 1:1-3 NLT) I have rejected sin, love your Word, and made it my lamp and light. Therefore, I am to prosper and produce continual fruit. Devil spirit of poverty, I rebuke you in Jesus' name. You must take your hands off my finances. I command you to move and be thrown into the sea now in the name of Jesus."

This is how to use your faith. Speak and command the Word of God into your life and situation. This is how God operates in faith.

> By faith we understand that the entire universe was formed at God's command, that what we now see did not come from anything that can be seen.
>
> — Hebrews 11:3 NLT

The Bible says God created the universe by faith, but what did this look like, practically? "Then God said, 'Let there be light,' and there was light." (Genesis 1:3) God used His faith by speaking. This is how you use your faith. When God was on the Earth as a man named Jesus, this is how He operated in faith.

> The next morning as they were leaving Bethany, Jesus was hungry. He noticed a fig tree in full leaf a little way off, so he went over to see if he could find any figs. But there were only leaves because it was too early in the season for fruit. Then Jesus said to the tree, "May no one ever eat your fruit again!" And the disciples heard him say it.
>
> — Mark 11:12-14 NLT

> The next morning as they passed by the fig tree he had cursed, the disciples noticed it had with-

ered from the roots up. Peter remembered
what Jesus had said to the tree on the previous
day and exclaimed, "Look, Rabbi! The fig tree
you cursed has withered and died!"

— Mark 11:20-21 NLT

How did Jesus handle the fig tree when it produced no fruit? Did
He say, "Peter, get the shovel?" No! Jesus spoke to the fig tree,
and it withered at the root! This was an act of faith because, in
the following passage, Jesus told them they could move mountains if they had the faith of God. Exercising faith in this
manner is modeled throughout the scriptures. You must first
believe in your heart, and from the faith that is in your heart,
you confess with your mouth.

But we continue to preach because we have the
same kind of faith the psalmist had when he
said, "I believed in God, so I spoke."

— 2 Corinthians 4:13 NLT

"A good person produces good things from the
treasury of a good heart, and an evil person
produces evil things from the treasury of an
evil heart. What you say flows from what is in
your heart."

— Luke 6:45 NLT

> If you openly declare that Jesus is Lord and believe
> in your heart that God raised him from the
> dead, you will be saved. For it is by believing in
> your heart that you are made right with God,
> and it is by openly declaring your faith that
> you are saved.
>
> — Romans 10:9-10 NLT

If you only believe in your heart and don't speak with your mouth, your faith will not work. If you only speak with your mouth and don't believe it in your heart, your faith will not work. You must saturate yourself in the Word of God and allow the Holy Spirit to breathe life into the Word in your heart. Then from your heart, you speak with the authority of Christ. You cannot be saved without following this process. You have to believe in your heart and also confess with your mouth. Why? This is how faith works. Begin to boldly speak out the revelations you hold in your heart. Speak these truths out in prayer, speak them out at work, and speak them out in the supermarket. Put your faith to work and begin seeing the promises of God come to pass in your life!

> "For assuredly, I say to you, whoever says to this
> mountain, 'Be removed and be cast into the
> sea,' and does not doubt in his heart, but
> believes that those things he says will be done,
> he will have whatever he says."
>
> — Mark 11:23 NKJV

Jesus said you can say something, and if you believe what you say and do not doubt, you will have what you say every time without exception. Begin to speak today! I will succeed and prosper. It is impossible for my bank account to run dry. I am healed. I will live and not die. I am anointed. I carry the power of the Holy Ghost. If you water the seed of faith in your life with confession, you will have what you say!

Write Bible confessions based on the Word and begin speaking them daily. Confess the Word of the Lord over your life every day in faith. Sometimes I confess a subject three times; sometimes, I make it once. What's the formula? There is no formula. You confess it until you believe the words coming out of your mouth. You will have what you say when you believe the things you say in faith.

Your Life Follows Your Words

> A man's stomach shall be satisfied from the fruit
> of his mouth; From the produce of his lips he
> shall be filled. Death and life are in the power
> of the tongue, And those who love it will eat
> its fruit.
>
> — Proverbs 18:20-21 NKJV

I remember when the Lord began revealing this to me. Your life won't be a product of your hard work, blood, sweat, and tears. What you have in life will not be a product of your efforts alone. Your life will be determined by the words that come from your mouth. What you have and don't have will be determined by your words. Your life will be filled by the words you speak. If you speak words of faith, your life will be filled with good things. If you speak words of unbelief, negativity, and ungratefulness, your life will be filled with negative things.

The difference between living and dying is the words you speak every day. You cannot prosper until you learn how to speak the right words and control your tongue. You cannot be used by God greatly and also be a negative or complaining person. You will have what you say, good or bad.

> We can make a large horse go wherever we want by means of a small bit in its mouth. And a small rudder makes a huge ship turn wherever the pilot chooses to go, even though the winds are strong. In the same way, the tongue is a small thing that makes grand speeches. But a tiny spark can set a great forest on fire.
>
> — James 3:3-5 NLT

In the same way, a thousand-pound animal is directed by a small bit in its mouth, and a small rudder steers a massive ship; your tongue sets the direction your life will go. Your life will not go where you want it to go. It will go in the direction you *tell* it to go. You are not subject to your environment. The passage above says, "And a small rudder makes a huge ship turn wherever the pilot chooses to go, even though the winds are strong." The wind doesn't determine the course of the ship. The storm does not determine the direction of the ship. A ship is directed through the strongest storms by a small rudder. You can move forward through anything if you set your course and command your life in the desired direction.

It doesn't matter if you grew up in a drug house in south Chicago or the bush in the heart of Africa. Your current circumstance will not bind you if you allow the Word of God to come alive in your heart and speak, commanding the world around you to align with the promises given in the Word of God. Settle the Word of God in your heart, and then use your words like a sword commanding the realities of Heaven to come into your life today.

> If you fully obey the Lord your God and carefully
>   keep all his commands that I am giving you
>   today, the Lord your God will set you high
>   above all the nations of the world. You will
>   experience all these blessings if you obey the
>   Lord your God: Your towns and your fields will
>   be blessed. Your children and your crops will
>   be blessed. The offspring of your herds and
>   flocks will be blessed. Your fruit baskets and
>   breadboards will be blessed. Wherever you go
>   and whatever you do, you will be blessed. The
>   Lord will conquer your enemies when they
>   attack you. They will attack you from one
>   direction, but they will scatter from you in
>   seven! The Lord will guarantee a blessing on
>   everything you do and will fill your storehouses

with grain. The Lord your God will bless you in the land he is giving you. If you obey the commands of the Lord your God and walk in his ways, the Lord will establish you as his holy people as he swore he would do. Then all the nations of the world will see that you are a people claimed by the Lord, and they will stand in awe of you. The Lord will give you prosperity in the land he swore to your ancestors to give you, blessing you with many children, numerous livestock, and abundant crops. The Lord will send rain at the proper time from his rich treasury in the heavens and will bless all the work you do. You will lend to many nations, but you will never need to borrow from them. If you listen to these commands of the Lord your God that I am giving you today, and if you carefully obey them, the Lord will make you the head and not the tail, and you will always be on top and never at the bottom. You must not turn away from any of the commands I am giving you today, nor follow after other gods and worship them.

— Deuteronomy 28:1-13 NLT

All praise to God, the Father of our Lord Jesus
    Christ, who has blessed us with every spiritual
    blessing in the heavenly realms because we are
    united with Christ.

                     — Ephesians 1:3 NLT

Don't forget that you Gentiles used to be
    outsiders. You were called "uncircumcised
    heathens" by the Jews, who were proud of
    their circumcision, even though it affected
    only their bodies and not their hearts. In those
    days you were living apart from Christ. You
    were excluded from citizenship among the
    people of Israel, and you did not know the
    covenant promises God had made to them.
    You lived in this world without God and
    without hope.

                     — Ephesians 2:11-12 NLT

And this is God's plan: Both Gentiles and Jews
    who believe the Good News share equally in
    the riches inherited by God's children. Both
    are part of the same body, and both enjoy the
    promise of blessings because they belong to
    Christ Jesus.

                     — Ephesians 3:6 NLT

Get the revelation! You have been brought into this promise of blessing God made with his children Israel by the blood of Jesus! This is for you today! Don't settle for anything less! Say it! I will prosper! I will have the most successful business in my town by the blessing of the Lord! I will not only work for my company, I will also run this company in Jesus' name! I will be the head! I'm rising higher in Jesus' name! I will never need a loan from a bank; God will give me cash to pay for the things I need! Any assignment against my life will fail; my enemies will try to attack me from one direction and then scatter in seven directions!

Get this revelation and speak it into every area of your life. This is how faith works. When the Devil comes and tries to put road-blocks in your life, don't settle for them. You have to get the promises rooted inside of you. Come to the place where you know what belongs to you and do not settle for anything less. When something comes into your life that contradicts what the Bible says about you and what belongs to you, do not accept it. Tell the mountain to move. If you have the faith of God, the mountain will be removed and cast into the sea! You must speak it for it to happen.

Bishop David Oyedepo said, "If it is too big for your mouth, it is too big for your hand." You cannot have what you do not call into existence by faith. If your mouth stays shut, your hand stays empty. I want to give you a Bible example of this.

> David replied to the Philistine, "You come to me
> with sword, spear, and javelin, but I come to
> you in the name of the Lord of Heaven's
> Armies—the God of the armies of Israel,

whom you have defied. Today the Lord will
conquer you, and I will kill you and cut off your
head. And then I will give the dead bodies of
your men to the birds and wild animals, and the
whole world will know that there is a God in
Israel! And everyone assembled here will know
that the Lord rescues his people, but not with
sword and spear. This is the Lord's battle, and
he will give you to us!" As Goliath moved closer
to attack, David quickly ran out to meet him.
Reaching into his shepherd's bag and taking
out a stone, he hurled it with his sling and hit
the Philistine in the forehead. The stone sank
in, and Goliath stumbled and fell face down on
the ground. So David triumphed over the
Philistine with only a sling and a stone, for he
had no sword. Then David ran over and pulled
Goliath's sword from its sheath. David used it
to kill him and cut off his head.

— 1 Samuel 17:45-50 NLT

Jonathan Shuttlesworth once said, "Before David ever killed
Goliath with a stone, he killed him with his words." This is how
faith works. You must call things into existence with the revelation of the authority given to you by Jesus.

(as it is written, "I have made you a father of many
nations") in the presence of Him whom he
believed—God, who gives life to the dead and

calls those things which do not exist as though
they did;

— Romans 4:17 NKJV

This is a key to the kingdom found throughout the Bible. Let's
look at another example from Abraham. Abraham was originally
called Abram; he was a very old man who had never had a single
child. Everything changed for him when God spoke to him in
Genesis.

> When Abram was ninety-nine years old, the Lord
> appeared to Abram and said to him, "I am
> Almighty God; walk before Me and be blame-
> less. And I will make My covenant between
> Me and you, and will multiply you exceeding-
> ly." Then Abram fell on his face, and God
> talked with him, saying: "As for Me, behold,
> My covenant is with you, and you shall be a
> father of]many nations. No longer shall your
> name be called Abram, but your name shall be
> Abraham; for I have made you a father of
> many nations. I will make you exceedingly
> fruitful; and I will make nations of you, and
> kings shall come from you."

— Genesis 17:1-6 NKJV

The name Abraham literally means father of many. Can you
imagine being Abram? You would have to introduce yourself as
the father of many; people would ask how many kids you have.

You would then have to reply, saying none. The person would then stare at you, wondering if you had looked in the mirror in the last seventy years. Abraham had to call his son Issac into existence by his faith. By speaking "father of many," he declared he would indeed have children, and many children at that.

He would not die without a son. Even though he was 100 years old, God would fulfill His promise. Let your spirit align with the Word of God and release your faith with your God-given authority. Begin to speak!

Pray Specific Prayers

The problem many people face with never getting the results of Bible faith is that they pray very vague and general prayers. This will never produce a harvest because faith is specific. In this section, I want to cover a few principles that will help you produce the fruit of faith.

> Now faith is the substance of things hoped for, the
> evidence of things not seen.
>
> — Hebrews 11:1 NKJV

For faith to produce anything, you must first identify what you are hoping for. Many people don't know what they want. When they look at their life, they know they are unsatisfied but don't know what change looks like. What are you hoping for? Until you can answer this question, your faith will lie dormant. Faith brings what you are hoping for into existence. If you are not hoping for anything, your faith has nothing to bring to life.

"I tell you, you can pray for anything, and if you
believe that you've received it, it will be yours."

— Mark 11:24 NLT

We can pray for anything. You must first identify what "any-thing" is before you can have it! This is a scriptural principle found throughout the ministry of Jesus. Blind Bartimaeus called out to Jesus and was met with the question, "What is it that you want?" He then responded, "I want to see." Bartimaeus had to verbalize and pinpoint what he wanted for his faith to kick in and bring forth his healing.

I love the story found in John 5. One day Jesus approached the pool of Bethesda when he met a sick man who had been ill for thirty-eight years. The sick were known to gather around the pool because many believed they would be healed if they were the first into the water. Jesus asks the man, "Would you like to be well?" This seems like a stupid question on the surface. Of course, he would like to be well; that is why he is at the pool. Jesus was no fool, yet He still asked this question. Why? For the man to receive healing, he first had to target his healing with his faith. By asking this question, Jesus got the man to target the thing he was desiring. The rest is history; the man was instantly healed, took his mat, and left the place of sickness.

Take delight in the Lord, and he will give you your
heart's desires.

— Psalm 37:4 NLT

Again, we see this same concept. You need desires in your heart, or the Lord has nothing to give you. Write out the things you are believing for and be specific. Do not just say, "Lord, bless me." When you wake up the next morning with air in your lungs, He has answered that prayer. How do you want the Lord to bless you? Do you mean physically? Financially? Materially? You need to be specific.

Let's say you meant financially. Now we are getting somewhere. Now you pray, "Lord, bless me financially." The next day, you walk down the street and find $5; the Lord answered your prayer. You may say, "Well, that's not exactly what I meant." You must say what you mean. How much per month do you want to increase? $500? $1,000?

Get specific. Once you get specific, your faith can work, bringing to pass the specific thing you are hoping for! You must see it in your heart before ever seeing it in your hand. Many people will take this as a formula and begin praying robotically. Yet, they do not really believe it or see it in their heart.

> "I tell you the truth, you can say to this mountain,
> 'May you be lifted up and thrown into the sea,'
> and it will happen. But you must really believe
> it will happen and have no doubt in your
> heart."
>
> — Mark 11:23 NLT

This passage tells us that faith means having the thing you hope for in your heart before you have it in your hand. Abraham had to see the stars and begin to assign faces to the stars before he could ever have a child. Jacob had to see the striped branches before seeing the striped livestock. You must have a clear vision in your spirit before faith can produce. Joseph dreamed of being in the position of a king before being placed in charge of ruling over Egypt. You must see the thing you are hoping for in your spirit before seeing it in your hand.

Believe God For a Plan

God works in specifics. Read back in Genesis how specific God was with Noah regarding the ark he was to build. God didn't only say to build a boat. He told Noah how big to build it, what to build it with, and what to put in it once he finished building it. Read back in Exodus at the instructions God gave for the tabernacle. God works in specifics.

When I became the pastor of our first church in Huntington, Texas, God spoke to me and told me to reach my city. That was very vague, so I went into a month of intermittent fasting and began asking the Lord for a plan. I said, "Lord, you know exactly what I need to do, when I need to do it, how I need to do it, where I need to do it, and who I need to do it with. Show me, Lord." Nothing came for several weeks. Then one afternoon, I was in prayer, and the Lord downloaded eight specific things in my spirit. Those specific instructions paved the way to a building, totally equipped for having a church, along with the money and no loan from a bank to purchase this property.

Pastor Gary Keesee once said many people have the "mailbox mentality." They work a $ 10-an-hour job and believe for $150,000 to show up in six days mysteriously in their mailbox. Can God do that? Yes! "All things are possible to the one who believes," Mark 9:23. God can absolutely do that, and there have been stories of God doing these things. But I want you to think differently. What does $150,000 really do? Does that help? Of course, it helps, but will that change your life? If $150,000 is a life-changing amount of money for you, I challenge you to begin dreaming God-sized dreams. Let's say you open your mailbox to $150,000; your life may change momentarily, but you will still go back to a job that only pays you $10 an hour.

You give a man a fish, and he eats for a day. You teach a man to fish, he eats for a lifetime. Have you ever heard this? God delights in giving people fish to eat for today, but He wants to go a step further and build structure into your life that ushers a continual flow of blessings. He doesn't just want to give you a pool full of water. He promises a river of living water that will spring from inside you (John 7:38). A river is guided by a river bed. God wants to open up streams, lanes, and avenues in your life that continually direct His blessings to flow into your possession.

When you pray, open your mind to receive a plan from the Holy Spirit. I love using Abraham as an example, considering he is the patriarch of our faith. When God promised to bless and multiply Abram, there was a method given by which the provision came. God taught Abram to dig water wells where his flocks and herds grew abundantly. This gave Abram the ability to monopolize the local industry.

The same was true for Jacob. God did not simply drop livestock into his lap. The Lord gave him a supernatural strategy to produce the livestock (Genesis 30).

Think back to when Peter first encountered Jesus. The encounter ended with Peter having two fishing boats full of fish, but did Jesus teleport those fish into Peter's boat? No, Jesus gave Peter instructions saying, "Go into the deep and let down your nets." (Luke 5:4) Jesus told Peter where to go and what to do. When we pray, we must open our minds to receive specific instructions from the Lord. Do not pray and simply hold your hand out.

> Your own ears will hear him. Right behind you a voice will say, "This is the way you should go," whether to the right or to the left.
>
> — Isaiah 30:21 NLT

God will give you a business idea, and once He gives you a business idea, He will tell you how to run your business by the Spirit and through His Word. The Holy Spirit will tell you which investments to make and when to make them. God will direct you in the endeavor He calls you into. Are you a stay-at-home mom? God will show you how to raise your kids by His Spirit and through His Word. He will tell you where they should go to school, what your children should watch, and what they should listen to. The Lord not only wants to bless you today; He wants to change your entire situation for generations to come.

> A good man leaves an inheritance to his children's children, But the wealth of the sinner is stored up for the righteous.
>
> — Proverbs 13:22 NKJV

God is trying to structure your life such that an avenue of blessing is still flowing in your family 80 years from now. Pray specific prayers and believe God for avenues that will usher in continual blessings. He will give you a plan.

Commit your actions to the Lord, and your plans
will succeed.

— Proverbs 16:3 NLT

Faith Doesn't Dream Small Dreams

"What do you mean, 'If I can'?" Jesus asked.
Anything is possible if a person believes."

— Mark 9:23 NLT

I can do all things through Christ who strengthens
me.

— Philippians 4:13 NKJV

It is impossible to have these scriptures sealed in your heart and not dream big dreams. How would you dream if there was no limit to how high you could ascend? How would you dream if money were not an issue? How would you dream if the word "impossible" was eliminated? This is the reality of dreaming with God. When God said, "nothing is impossible if you can believe it," He absolutely meant it. One of the most frustrating things I have come across is children dreaming dreams bound by the chains of realism.

I spent several years in youth ministry and have had many conversations with kids about what they want to do when they grow up. The conversation usually went like this.

"Hey, little Jimmy, what do you want to do when you graduate?"

"Well, I think I want to be a welder."

"Really now, and why is that?"

"Well, welders make $200,000 a year."

It was the same song with a different melody, depending on the kid I asked. "I want to be a welder, I want to be a nurse, and I want to be a physical therapist." These things are great! We need all these things for society to function correctly. God can call welders to the west Texas pipelines and nurses to the delivery rooms of hospitals. My problem was never with the answers I received; my problem was with the reasons for the responses.

Every answer was driven by a dollar amount and never by the voice of the Lord. People dream too small. Their idea of a dream is a certain car, a certain house, or a certain amount of money in the bank. Therefore, they choose life paths that, in theory, should allow them to achieve their dreams but fall short of their potential. I understand the motive. It is great to desire a good life and to want to take care of your family. I wish more men today would step up and take care of their families, but the issue is the small-mindedness and unbelief rooted in that way of thinking. Many people think like animals. Animals do not dream of changing the world; animals live to survive. Animals don't think about the generations to come. Animals wake up, eat, survive, and repeat. So many people live with that same mindset.

People believe they must choose between following the call of God and living a good life. This couldn't be farther from the truth. Everything you do in life should be because the Lord told you. If you are a coal miner, it should be because God told you to be one. If someone asked you today, "Why do you live where you live? Why do you work where you work? Why do you go to church where you go to church?" The answer should be a story of how the Holy Spirit spoke to your heart and instructed you in all of the listed areas. If that is not true for you, your life is out of alignment.

Many people settle for a small life where no one knows their name, rooted in ignorance, doubt, and unbelief about the will of God regarding their provision. If God calls you to be a school-teacher, you will be more physically, financially, and materially blessed being a schoolteacher than being a lawyer in New York City. Your most blessed place is where the Lord tells you to be. People have dreams, but they must bring them back to "reality" because some backslidden, backwoods preacher told them they needed a "real plan" in life. "You are called to preach, you say? Well, you better get a plan B because you'll never support a family that way." The Bible doesn't tell us to seek after the means needed to live our lives and, if there's time, serve the kingdom of God on the side. Jesus said the opposite.

> "But seek first the kingdom of God and His right-
> eousness, and all these things shall be added to
> you."
>
> — Matthew 6:33 NKJV

What 'things' will be added to you? Your clothes, food, and everything required to live a functioning life. Jesus tells us in Matthew 6 to "not worry about the things of everyday life." He said that this is the way unbelievers live and think. If we have faith and "seek first the kingdom of God and live righteously," everything people kill themselves trying to get, in the hustle and bustle, will be added to our lives. Be who God has called you to be. Do what the Lord has called you to do. Train your kids to know this promise of provision so they will dream without limitations.

Once you understand that God promises to meet your needs, if you will serve His kingdom and carry out His purposes, you can begin to dream God-sized dreams. You won't be concerned with the things that bind many others to live small lives where their biggest goal is the white picket fence and the dog in the yard. If you obey the Lord and go where He calls you to go and do what He calls you to do, He will give you the white picket fence and the dog for free. All while the world kills itself, in its own strength, trying to obtain what the Lord has already promised you.

What most people consider their ceiling—having their needs taken care of—is your floor if you will believe the Word of the Lord. Never dream about how you can make enough to have a good life. Dream about changing a city. Dream about seeing abortion eradicated. Dream about seeing the public school system completely restructured. Your goal should be to impact this world in whatever field you are called to. When you die, the world should feel it. Get it in your spirit that God is not just a 'bills paid and a roof over your head' type of God. Our father is not a God of just enough. The God of the Bible is "El-Shaddai," the God who is more than enough. Jesus's first miracle was turning water into wine (John 2). Not just any wine, but the choicest wine, the absolute best. Not only the best wine, but he turned six water-pots of stone that held 30 gallons apiece. That is 180 gallons of the purest, most wonderful wine. More wine than those people could drink in a year. Why? 'First things' are important in the Bible. Jesus did this as His first miracle because He wanted to make a statement. I AM El-Shaddai. I AM the God of abundance.

When Jesus called Peter in Luke 5, He caused two of Peter's fishing boats to be so full of fish that they began to sink. Why? Jesus was making an important first impression. I AM the God of abundance. Come and follow me. Money? No problem. Food? No problem. When Jesus fed the 5,000 (plus women and children) in Luke 9, with only a few loaves of bread and a few fish, the Bible says everyone ate as much as they wanted. Jesus didn't have to feed anyone, but He did. He could have multiplied the bread and fish to be just enough for them not to die in the wilderness, but He took it a step further and gave them more than enough.

The Bible says, "they ate until they were full." (Luke 9:17) The most interesting thing to me is found in verse 17, where the Bible says, "and afterward, the disciples picked up twelve baskets of leftovers!" There are many points to be made about the leftovers. Maybe they were given to the boy who sowed his bread and fish. Maybe they were kept by the twelve disciples as a reward for serving the kingdom. One thing I know for certain is Jesus was making a statement with this miracle. I AM El-Shadaai. Jesus made it very clear, time and time again, that our God is the God of abundant provision.

Do not let provision be your reason for doing or not doing what God has called you to do. He will provide, and He will provide abundantly if you have faith to believe it and receive it. Dream big dreams that are not limited by the burdens of this world. If it's God's will, it's God's bill. He will always fund anything and everything He has called you to do.

Chapter Seven

Practical Steps to Develop Your Faith

When learning about spiritual things, you find many things are quite practical; not everything is a heavy, deep theological revelation. When it comes to developing faith, most people are clueless. When asking for help, they receive an answer deeper than the grand canyon, leaving them more confused than they were to begin with. I am a practical person— an A, B, C, 1, 2, 3 type of person. I want to give you very simple tools that, when implemented, will cause your faith to grow and flourish. Faith that shakes a nation and marks your name in the history books is not simply caught in a meeting. Faith that reaches a generation develops day in and day out through spiritual discipline.

"You will only go as far as your spiritual discipline allows you."

— Ted Shuttlesworth, Jr.

You won't go where you want to go in life; you will go where you train yourself to go in life.

It has come to my attention that many people serving in church ministry are pulled away from the normal Sunday or midweek service. These are the workers who minister to the kids and run the lights and computers. Sometimes these people burn out and grow cold. Many blame this on not being fed. I truly understand what they are saying, but let me ask: Who preaches to the preacher? How does the one doing the teaching, week in and week out, stay on fire, constantly growing and full of fresh revelation, even though they are not sitting in a weekly church meeting being fed? This is the thought I have been pondering. How is this done?

Spiritual Disciplines

You must develop four key disciplines in your life. Before we get to the practical steps you must take to grow your faith, I need you to understand a few things. The fire of God, the anointing, the presence, the goosebumps, or cold chills—however you want to describe it—do not automatically stay in your life. You must tend to it. Many people wonder what is wrong with them; they go to an anointed meeting and get all fired up, but in a few weeks, the feeling fades, and they lose what they received. Why? They did not tend the flame.

> I remember your genuine faith, for you share the
> faith that first filled your grandmother Lois
> and your mother, Eunice. And I know that
> same faith continues strong in you. This is why

> I remind you to fan into flames the spiritual
> gift God gave you when I laid my hands
> on you.
>
> — 2 Timothy 1:5-6 NLT

In this passage, Paul tells Timothy to fan the flames. Why? If you don't fan the flames, it will go out. The fire of God in your life is like a natural fire. You can have a large bonfire raging, but the fire diminishes as the night goes on. You find only a few red embers when you wake up the next morning. You must throw wood on the fire to keep it raging; you must get oxygen to the fire to get a flame. Many people have great encounters and then leave their fire untended, and the flame goes out. This is why you need spiritual discipline in your life. Every day you must throw logs on the fire; every day you must take off your hat and fan the flame. As you do, the fire is not only sustained, but it also grows and consumes every part of your being.

Read the Word of God Every Day

The first spiritual discipline you must adopt today is the daily intake of the Word of God. Yes, I'll say that again...daily. There were many great things that I learned while in Bible college. I learned lessons in doctrine and theology. I learned about Jews and Gentiles. I learned big words, like transubstantiation, but the most beneficial thing I received while in Bible college was not the lessons in theology—although they were valuable—the most beneficial thing I came home with was spiritual disciplines.

Your opinion on Calvinism versus Arminianism will not carry you forward in the future. But the disciplines you create in your life will facilitate continued growth and development. While in Bible college, I took a class requiring me to read the Bible daily. Three chapters a day and five on Sunday. This class literally changed my life. When you do this for two years, you form a habit, and when you make that habit a priority, you form a discipline. Sadly, a few short years after finishing Bible College, many people I went to school with dropped off the map and quit following the Lord altogether. I'm willing to bet, for each of these individuals, if you looked at their lives, you would find that they veered off the path when they stopped reading the Bible consistently. Your flame will go out if you are not in the Word daily.

Jesus said he did not live off of bread alone, but by every word that proceeded from the mouth of the Father (Matthew 4:4). When Jesus spoke this, He was referencing the manna from Heaven that sustained the children of Israel in the wilderness. God did not give them manna to eat once a week; He gave them manna to eat every day. Jesus tied this together with receiving fresh revelation from the Father in the form of the Word of God every day. You can't live off of last week's word. You can't live off of last year's revelation. You can't live off of an experience 35 years ago in a Revival meeting. You must read the Word daily and allow the Holy Spirit to use it to teach you every day.

When you read the Bible daily, you are guaranteed to prosper spiritually. Jesus said, "Keep on asking, and you will receive what you ask for. Keep on seeking, and you will find. Keep on knocking, and the door will be opened to you." (Matthew 7:7) There will be days when you don't feel like seeking, but when you decide to read the Word of God every day without compromise, you will find Jesus. When you create structure in your life where you are constantly seeking, you will find. Do not wait until your feelings tell you to seek God. If you do that, all it takes is one bad day, then one bad day turns into a week, and a week turns into a month. Before you know it, you are miles from where you began, and you don't even know how you got there.

Things become foggy in life when you get away from the Word of God. The Bible says in Psalms 119 that the Word of God is a lamp unto my feet and the light unto my path. That means everything in life must filter through the Word.

When you get away from the Word, you start filtering life through your senses; what you see, feel, hear, or experience. Senses tell you a different report than what the Word of God says if you allow them. When you get away from the Word, you start filtering life through what Facebook, Fox, or even CNN says. If you allow these things to become your lamp and your light, you will find yourself in a pit of doubt, unbelief, and despair.

> "Be strong and very courageous. Be careful to obey
> all the instructions Moses gave you. Do not
> deviate from them, turning either to the right
> or to the left. Then you will be successful in
> everything you do. Study this Book of Instruc-
> tion continually. Meditate on it day and night
> so you will be sure to obey everything written
> in it. Only then will you prosper and succeed
> in all you do. This is my command—be strong
> and courageous! Do not be afraid or discour-

> aged. For the Lord your God is with you wher-
> ever you go."
>
> —Joshua 1:7-9 NLT

God told Joshua to keep His Word before his eyes and not deviate from it. God promised Joshua that if he did this, he would be successful and prosper. This was contingent upon keeping the Word before his eyes and ensuring he did not deviate from it. This promise is true for us. We can prosper, we can succeed, we can rule in life and not be ruled by life, BUT we must also keep the Word before our eyes so we don't deviate from it. You are doing this when you build the discipline of studying the Word of God every day. You will see life differently as you read God's Word with the Holy Spirit. As your mind begins to change, you are transformed. As you are transformed, your life is transformed.

You will never grow apart from the Word of God. You'll only grow as much as your revelation and faith allow you. Revelation and faith come by the Word of God. As you continually read God's Word, you will receive continual revelation. You will come across a line or a passage where the light bulb comes on, and your mind opens to the reality of what God has given you. Now faith comes by the Word of God, and you have thrown another log on the fire in your heart.

There are infinite benefits to reading the Bible every day. Building the discipline of reading the Bible daily guarantees you will uncover your purpose on this earth. When it comes to your calling, your purpose, and the plan God has for your life, people are always looking for a sign in the clouds. People are always waiting for an angel of the Lord to appear and tell them their purpose. More people are looking for confirmation in their soy latte instead of looking in the Word of God. Where do you receive revelation about your specific purpose? Can God speak to you through angels? Can Jesus appear to you in a dream? Well, He can, but this will not be the case for 99.9% of the instruction you receive throughout your life. Your specific purpose will be revealed to you by burdens formed from reading the Word of God and allowing the Holy Spirit to speak to your heart.

> My ambition has always been to preach the Good
> News where the name of Christ has never
> been heard, rather than where a church has
> already been started by someone else. I have
> been following the plan spoken of in the Scrip-
> tures, where it says, "Those who have never
> been told about him will see, and those who
> have never heard of him will understand."
>
> — Romans 15:20-21

Paul received revelation about what he was to do on the Earth through reading the scriptures. As he read the scriptures, the Holy Ghost grabbed ahold of those verses and smacked Paul over the head with them. And Paul said, "Oh my gosh, this is what I must do. I must go tell people." Stop looking to the clouds and start digging into the Word. As you do this, the Holy Ghost will burden your heart, and your specific purpose will materialize before your eyes.

Paul was not the only one. Jesus also received instruction about His earthly ministry through the scriptures.

> When he came to the village of Nazareth, his boyhood home, he went as usual to the synagogue on the Sabbath and stood up to read the Scriptures. The scroll of Isaiah the prophet was handed to him. He unrolled the scroll and found the place where this was written: "The Spirit of the Lord is upon me, for He has anointed me to bring Good News to the poor, He has sent me to proclaim that captives will be released, that the blind will see, that the oppressed will be set free, and that the time of the Lord's favor has come." He rolled up the scroll, handed it back to the attendant, and sat down. All eyes in the synagogue looked at him intently. Then he began to speak to them. "The Scripture you've just heard has been fulfilled this very day!"
>
> — Luke 4:16-21

I imagine Jesus as a teenager listening to a rabbi read from the prophet Isaiah and coming to this prophetic part about Jesus and Jesus having the classic human being lightbulb moment. "This is talking about me. I now see what I must do." Years later, He stands in a synagogue and declares to the people what He has been sent to do, according to the scriptures. I don't know a single person who has read the Bible every day for the last year and still struggles with the question "What am I to do on the

Earth?" From this discipline of reading the Word every day, and by the Holy Spirit, you will walk in step with the plan God prepared for you.

Prayer

The discipline of prayer is the second spiritual discipline you need to adopt today to develop your faith and keep the flame of the Holy Ghost burning hotter and not diminishing. I use the word discipline because there will be times your flesh doesn't want to pray; ask the disciples in the garden of Gethsemane. Just because you don't want to, that doesn't mean you don't need to. People forget that we are in a relationship with God. There are different forms of prayer. You have intercessory prayer, praying in the Spirit, and engaging in spiritual warfare through prayer.

People get so busy that they neglect fellowship with the Father. Don't get me wrong, all these forms of prayer are extremely important and necessary. It is vital to do the work of the Father, but we must certainly not forsake our fellowship with Him. Prayer is a conversation. How many people speak in a conversation? —more than one unless you're a "Karen." Most of the time, we do not have conversations with God, we simply wait until all hell is breaking loose, and then we run to Him screaming our requests, begging Him to help us. Once we have stated our case, we hang up the phone and hope for an answer; that is not fellowship with God and not effective praying. It is wonderful to make our requests known when we come boldly into His throne room, but we often hang up the line before the Holy Spirit can answer us. We must create space in our lives for the Holy Spirit to speak to us.

I have consistently read through the Gospels over and over. I finish in John and start again in Matthew. My goal has been to immerse myself in the life and ministry of Jesus. I am blown away by what He modeled for us in the scriptures regarding prayer. You repeatedly read where Jesus retreated to a private place to pray. What did He know that many of us do not? Jesus understood the importance of prayer in a person's life and how crucial it is for sustainability. Jesus was not only close to God; He was God. If He had to constantly withdraw to a quiet place away from the busyness of the world to pray, what makes me think I don't need to do that as well?

> Come and listen to my counsel. I'll share my heart
> with you and make you wise.
>
> — Proverbs 1:23 NLT

People don't understand that God is not just a taskmaster. He is a loving father who wants to share His heart with you. God doesn't need anything by nature. God did not create minions in Adam and Eve; He created a family to have fellowship with. The Father wants to fellowship with you in the spirit. We grow cold and hard when we begin to do the work of a distant God whom we do not know. You are not only working for God, but you are also working with God. We are partners and joint heirs. The Holy Spirit is not a demon; He doesn't possess people and force them into action. No, He partners with us, with our faith, and with our action.

Church

> And let us not neglect our meeting together, as
> some people do, but encourage one another,
> especially now that the day of his return is
> drawing near.
>
> — Hebrews 10:25 NLT

Consistently attending church is the third discipline I want you to adopt today. The best decision you can make today is to stop treating the commands of the Bible like suggestions. The Bible does not suggest going to church; it commands us to do so. If you're not going to Church on the Lord's day, you're not living for Him the other six days of the week. People say they don't need to attend church to be a Christian. Do you think the people saying this are in the streets winning the lost and healing the sick? No. From my experience, they are spiritual flakes and weirdos, too busy eating Krispy Kremes and smoking cigarettes to do anything in life, much less come to church once a week.

There are two reasons why a Christian doesn't go to church. One, they are lazy and don't make it a priority in their life. Two, they are spiritually rebellious and disobey the Lord's authority and earthly leaders' authority. Stay away from these people. Most of the time, these are the weirdos who have bounced around every place in town and are holding their own meetings in their mom's garage because their knowledge is superior. There are many things to not be legalistic about but going to church is not one of them. Decide today: when other Christians are gathering, you will be there.

> All the believers devoted themselves to the apos-
> tles' teaching, and to fellowship, and to sharing
> in meals (including the Lord's Supper, and to
> prayer.)

> — Acts 2:42 NLT

> Seek the Kingdom of God above all else, and live
> righteously, and he will give you everything you
> need.

> — Matthew 6:33 NLT

The early church devoted itself to the gathering of the saints. They didn't build their schedule, and when they were free, they showed up. Everything in life revolved around the believers gathering. Don't make plans on Sundays. Don't make plans on Wednesdays. Put church first, put the body of Christ first, and build the rest of your schedule around the gathering of believers. If you're on vacation, you're visiting a church where you are.

> But the godly will flourish like palm trees and
> grow strong like the cedars of Lebanon. For
> they are transplanted to the Lord's own house.
> They flourish in the courts of our God. Even
> in old age they will still produce fruit. they will
> remain vital and green.

> — Psalm 92:12-14 NLT

There are blessings for being rooted in the house of the Lord. Take this scripture and begin to stand on it. If you plant yourself in the house of the Lord, you will flourish. In old age, you will have your health, and you will be continually fruitful.

> Don't you realize that all of you together are the
> temple of God and that the Spirit of God lives
> in you?
>
> — 1 Corinthians 3:16 NLT

The Bible says that you are the temple of the Holy Ghost as an individual, but also collectively, we are the temple of the Holy Ghost. What does this mean? You carry the presence as an individual, but there is another presence when we are together in one place in one accord. You can't get everything alone. There are certain things you can only get in an anointed meeting where believers are gathered.

> Now these are the gifts Christ gave to the church:
> the apostles, the prophets, the evangelists, and
> the pastors and teachers. Their responsibility
> is to equip God's people to do his work and
> build up the church, the body of Christ.
>
> — Ephesians 4:11-12 NLT

You can't do this alone. People who say that you don't need a church to be a Christian are the same people who never study the Bible. The five-fold ministry gifts are given to build up the Church. As stated earlier, God works through men and women.

When God wants something done, he sends a man or a woman. This is how God speaks and ministers to His body. When Christians need a shepherd, God uses a man as a pastor. When Christians need teaching, God uses a man as a teacher to teach the Church. There are certain things that you will only receive through the deposit God has placed inside of someone else. There is a revelation waiting for you on the lips of another person. To exclude yourself from church is to exclude yourself from growth. You cannot be a mountain-moving Christian and at the same time a Christian who doesn't attend church.

Signs of a Good and Bad Church

When I moved to the small town of Huntington, Texas, the sign said the population was 2,100 people. To my amazement, I saw a church on every street corner. There are well over 60 churches in the small town of 2,100 people. I asked myself the question, "Are all these churches from the Lord? Did God plant all these churches?" I believe some people are called and sent, and some people just buy a microphone and go. I asked, "Who is planted here by you, Father? Who is doing something?" The church you go to is the third most important decision you will ever make in your life. The first is receiving Jesus Christ. The second is the person you marry. The third is the church you go to. The church you go to is the difference between dying rich or dying poor, your marriage flourishing or suffering multiple divorces, your kids receiving the fire of God and serving the Lord, or them coming home from university with a same-sex partner and a nose ring.

Build your life around a good church. I had a family member tell me that there are no good churches nearby. At one time, my response would have been, "That's probably a lazy excuse for not going to church." After 2020 I saw the truth in that statement. Now, my response is, "Move!" We live in a time where you can make money in millions of different ways. It doesn't take a month on the back of a wagon to travel between states. A solid, faith-filled church, full of the power of God, is worth moving for.

When you put the kingdom first in your life and make the things of God your top priority, everything in life will be added to you. How can I tell if a church is good or bad? If a church shut down in 2020-2021, that is a red flag.

There are only two reasons a church shut down in 2020. One, they listened to the false prophets of CNN and feared a virus with a 99.8% survival rate. Even if the survival rate was 50%, why would you let a person who doesn't believe what the Bible says teach you and your family? If you're wondering what I am talking about, read Psalms 91, and believe it for what it says. A church needs a solid leader, not someone's puppet. They may say that the government threatened them, but who should we obey? Man or God (Acts 5:29)?

Two, many so-called Christian leaders were not really afraid of the virus. Many people who closed their churches were marching in the streets with Black Lives Matter. Why? Their ministry is a business that serves people in the wrong ways. Many of these leaders shut their doors because they knew if they didn't, many of their liberal members would ask, "How can you still be open? We will be going elsewhere."

In the minds of weak leaders, people leaving means losing money, so they shut down. Again, many of these same people were in the streets marching with Black Lives Matter. Why? Did they suddenly get political and become activists? No. They knew that if they didn't get behind what the ladies on The View were barking, half of their liberal congregation would be out the door. That's not a man of God; that's a businessman putting on Christian circus shows. Again, if a church shut down in 2020, I question the true reason.

Another thing to look for is whether a church goes after the lost. My motto is, "Win the lost, at all cost." If a church is simply a Christian country club that allocates all its funds to enhance the Sunday experience and is not in the community going after the lost, I would not attend that church. When you go to a church, you should receive constant teaching and training to be a soul winner. This is God's top priority, and the call of God to every Christian (Mark 16:15). Win the lost. A church disconnected from winning souls is a church disconnected from the heart of God.

Does the church preach the Bible? If you go to a service that is 40 minutes of music and a 20-minute sermon based on one scripture to make an irrelevant point, then you are in the wrong place. Faith comes by hearing the Word (Romans 10:17). Faith doesn't come by singing songs; faith comes by hearing the Word of God. Without faith, it is impossible to please God (Hebrews 11:6). God wants faith preached and activated in His people. The word and ministry of the Holy Ghost is the most important part of a service. Oftentimes, Christianity erroneously caters to people who are not interested in God. You can't preach for more than 30 minutes, and if services are more than 1 ½ hours, people won't come back a second time. If this is the kind of chatter happening in a staff meeting, get out now. If people are not getting activated and launched, then the church is not preaching faith.

Does the church minister through the laying on of hands? Laying on of hands is not an insignificant practice of Christianity. Jesus laid hands on people to bless, cast out devils, and heal the sick. Paul laid hands on people to get them baptized in the Holy Ghost. Jesus told us that we could lay our hands on people and do the same works He did (Mark 16:17, Acts 19). When a church classifies its ministry time as an open altar where a line of men and women lay hands on people and pray faithless prayers with no authority, the church has no understanding of the gifts of the Spirit and impartation. "Your prayers are as good as my prayers." This could potentially be true if prayed from a place of understanding and faith. The reality is prayers are not all the same most of the time. Sadly, most people on the "prayer team" can not even explain the fundamentals of the Gospel if asked. Get into a good faith teaching church that will set you and your family on the path to greatness.

Chapter Eight

Spiritual Mentorship

Walk with the wise and become wise; associate
with fools and get in trouble.

— Proverbs 13:20 NLT

And the Lord came down in the cloud and spoke
to Moses. Then he gave the seventy elders the
same Spirit that was upon Moses. And when
the Spirit rested upon them, they prophesied.
But this never happened again.

— Numbers 11:25 NLT

> This is why I remind you to fan into flames the
> spiritual gift God gave you when I laid my
> hands on you.
>
> — 2 Timothy 1:6 NLT

This last piece of advice is not necessarily a discipline but a matter of life placement. You need to place your life under spiritual leadership. People who live outside of spiritual authority and leadership are often loose-living weirdos. Many people go to church without submitting to mentorship. A friend once told me that a pastor should be able to speak correction without losing members—losing members is the reality in most cases.

Spiritual mentorship is key to growth and acceleration. You can't have what you don't sit under. In every area of life, you need someone who successfully does what you want to do, and you must place yourself under them. If you want to be a real estate millionaire, you need to connect with someone who has successfully done what you endeavor to do. If you want skinny jeans and smoke machines, you will place yourself under that flow. If you want to be a word of faith teacher, you need to sit under Kenneth Hagin's and Kenneth Copeland's ministries. Listen to what they say, read their books, and study how they did what they did. You will become what you surround yourself with. If you walk with the wise, you will become wise. Statistically, you will make the median income of the five people you spend the most time with. Theoretically, you could become a millionaire by changing the people you spend time with. How? Most of life is a mindset. The only thing that limits a person is that person's belief about their own capability. Nothing is impossible for the one who believes (Mark 9:23).

When you get around people who have done it, or are doing it, your mind grabs ahold of the reality of what you can do. "As a man thinks in his heart so he is." (Proverbs 23:7) Knowledge is wealth and success. "For a lack of knowledge people perish." (Hosea 4:6) If you want to do what someone is doing, you need to know what they know. How can you know what they know? Be humble and ask. Knock, seek, and you will find. Do less talking and more listening. Pride is the kryptonite of success. When you think you know it all, you are an utter fool.

There is always someone who knows more than you do and is doing more than you are. Instead of being intimidated, learn and receive what took them a lifetime to learn. Let someone's ceiling be your floor, and one day let your ceiling be someone else's floor. This is the heart of discipleship.

You will always have coffee-shop experts, the guys who spend hours discussing what you should do with your money and investments yet have no skin in the game. Don't listen to these people. If what they say works, why hasn't it worked for them? If I don't like the fruit, I'm not eating from the tree. A good rule to live by is if someone has not successfully done twice what you're trying to do, they have no right telling you how to do it once.

Pick your mentors wisely. Don't tie your life to someone who is simply a philosopher with great theories. Many people spend their entire life betting on the wrong racehorse. If you're a forty-five-year-old pastor and God has yet to give you a building and a church, I don't want to hear your theories on running a church.

You're as qualified to give church advice as I am to give astrophysics advice.

There will be people that read this and get offended, but it doesn't change the facts. This is what I mean by humility. Humble yourself and come under someone who has done it and let them help you. God will use you. You need leaders in your life whom you trust to see things you don't see. A person who is deceived doesn't know it. If they did know it, they wouldn't be deceived, they would be stupid.

Submit to leaders who can point to things you may genuinely not see. I was on a phone call with a mentor of mine, and he was giving me a list of things I needed to change. This was not offensive to me; it was music to my ears. I implemented the changes and saw an immediate increase. Everyone is so afraid of being corrected. If that is you, be prepared to stay small. When God corrects, it is because He wants to take you higher and give you more.

Learn to love wisdom. Learn to seek after it like hidden treasure. You can't make disciples if you've never been a disciple. You can't be a teacher if you've never been a student. If you think no one does it like you and you have nothing but critical things to say about everyone and their dog, you are living in utter foolishness, and God can't use you.

Some people criticize Joel Osteen. How about you pastor a church of 40,000 people and get into the homes of millions each week, then you can talk. Until then, realize that you're still in the same place that you were five years ago because God resists the proud but gives grace to the humble.

Afterword

This book is not the entirety of the faith doctrine meticulously exegete into a one-thousand-page masterpiece. This book simply peels the curtain back to the message and power of faith. I want people to get a hold of this material and develop a solid starting point for their life of faith.

As you read this book, I pray your spirit begins to dream, and your expectation rises. I pray you truly believe that nothing is impossible for you and that the God of the Bible is still alive, and well, and answering your prayers offered in faith. By faith, you will take new ground. You will accomplish more in this one year than you did in the previous five, and it will happen with ease. Faith will make it easy; the anointing will make the impossible very much possible.

I pray that the box you live in is completely obliterated. Jesus will no longer be a historical figure from a book, but you will know His power and see His very real blessing flowing in your life. The time is now! Get going, get moving, and by faith, you will possess every promise that God has given to you!

About the Author

Johnathan Wallace founded Revival House Ministries International and launched Revival House Church in January 2022, along with his wife, Karissa Wallace. Revival House Ministries International is a ministry dedicated to teaching this generation about the kingdom of God and releasing the flame of revival to the nations. Revival House Church is planted in the heart of East Texas and serves the community of Angelina County.

www.rhctx.com

 facebook.com/rhctx

CPSIA information can be obtained
at www.ICGtesting.com
Printed in the USA
BVHW040705141222
654205BV00002B/30